sitting in the unknown

a collection of poems for military loved ones

sarah curtis

for more information,
email contact@amilitarywifeslife.com

ISBN: 979-8-218-23752-3

cover design: Lillian Hatfield M.Ed.
interior illustrations: Sarah Curtis

https://amilitarywifeslife.com

to Chase, I love you

to my fellow military loved ones, I see you

and to my Heavenly Father, I trust you

author's note

This book started as a personal journal. A way for
me to articulate my confusing emotions during our
first deployment cycle.

These poems were yanked straight from my heart
to my notebook like magnets. The words needed
to be written, if not for anyone else to read, then at
least for me to write. To process, feel, understand
and survive.

You are holding a piece of my heart.

So whatever season you find yourself in, whether
that be surviving, living, or thriving, I pray that
these words bring you comfort and validation.

You are not alone.

I, too, am sitting in the unknown.

seasons

surviving

In order to accept the unknown,
we must first
sit with it

I'm sick and tired
of rescheduling
cancelling
missing
important moments
that may only happen once

As someone who
thrives
and blooms
with steady plans,
I often find myself
wilting

When do I start
sharing
the changes that
might happen
in our transient military lives?

Even I
get disappointed.

Explaining our changed plans
is almost as hard
as the changed plans themselves

13

Why can't I accept
that parts of my life
simply aren't in my
control?

An emotion
I didn't expect
within military life
was grief.

Grief over shared loss.

Over being left behind.

Over not having answers
missing family
being alone

Finding a
new normal
sucks
when your normal
never stays the same

16

One day I'll be whole
but for now
my heart is beating
on the other side of the world

A timid voice
echoes through my soul,
whispering
begging
"please bring them back home"

Our home has taken on
a new kind of rhythm.

Not one
of joy or sadness,
anger or resentment,
but rather
everything at once,
each emotion
fighting
for our attention.

And yet,
despite the constant
noise,
our hearts
steadily beat
to the sound of
longing,
aching for your
steady rhythm

You can hear
the space
between us.

The distance
empties our minds
and hollows our conversation

The constant
goings
and comings
make my heart
my soul
my very being
ache

I don't want
to find a new normal
without you,
but it's a need
required for survival

One day your biggest concern is when they'll be
home for dinner.

Then a week goes by
and suddenly
you need to plan a move
prepare for a deployment
say goodbye to your closest friend
and find a new normal
again

At first
it's a gentle curiosity,
and a reminder
that you're grateful for what you have.

But then
it festers
and feeds
and if you allow it
to grow out of control
it consumes you.

It's simply a question of when

      - jealousy

There's a blurry haze
between necessary
and destructive
comparison.

On one side,
you gauge
how your experience compares
to others.

On the other side,
you drop down into a deep
well of pity.
And when you finally land at the bottom,
you're in too deep to
climb out

Why is it
that all my friends leave
and grow
and I'm stuck here
lonely
with no place to go?

There are times
when your village surrounds you
engulfs you
and lifts you to your feet.

But there are also times
when you desperately need them,
yet no one reaches out
to offer support.

These times are the hardest
because not only
are you
trudging through darkness,
but you're doing it
alone

She claims that she'll accept you
exactly as you are.
She says she'll understand, too,
and soothe your every scar.

So you tell her how you're feeling
and decide to not hold back.
Your heart still can't find healing
and she nods as you unpack.

She shares about the days
when she felt all this, but more.
She tells you all the ways
that your life you should adore.

And as the chat moves along,
your heart begins to ache.
You start to think "I must be wrong.
My feelings are a mistake."

And as the conversation ends,
you're raw and shattered and weak.
You wonder why your pain offends.
"Why did I even speak?"

My military journey
has been a
downpour of rain
and chaotic wind
with no time to breathe.

But then I look at
the hurricane
tornado
tidal wave
of someone else's journey,
and feel like
I shouldn't be allowed
to call mine
bad weather

When I first got a glimpse of the future,
I was drawn
to her perfection,
which I desperately
wanted to absorb.

But just beyond that glimpse
was the beauty
of the imperfect present,
disintegrating
as I chose to ignore
the only reality
I'll ever be able to reach.

I got so caught up in the idea of the future
that I forgot to live
today

"This is not forever"
as we say goodbye once more.
"This is not forever"
while I'm sobbing on the floor.

"This is not forever"
as I hang up the phone.
"This is not forever"
while I lay in bed alone.

This is not forever, yes,
but you must still learn how
to breathe and function and survive.
Because
it is
now

Working on me
is not a luxury
but a need
that my body
and mind
demand

There's a prick of time
somewhere between the aching
and the peace
that is guilt.

When it's allowed to linger,
is given space
and made comfortable,
that prick of time
stretches
and pulls
and yanks
until it's so enveloping that
guilt
is all you can see.

And you are left
torn and
broken,
stuck in this
vastness
that is guilt

Why do I feel that
anyone else
in my position
wouldn't struggle like I am?

Why
in my problem-solving mind
can I not just
be?

Why must I always
do?

Sitting in the unknown is a conscious choice.

Choosing to feel instead of ignore.
Choosing to feel instead of act.
Choosing to feel instead of fix.

And it hurts.

It hurts to allow those feelings in.
It hurts to feel instead of to act.
It hurts to find patience in yourself when every
inch of you is
restless.

It hurts to do nothing.

But sometimes that is the only option.

And sometimes giving yourself that space
and succumbing to inaction
provides you with the
very answers you needed
all along

There is strength in simply
being.

By existing,
you are making the most
important decision of all

words that I'm
tired of hearing

Look on the bright side

At least it's not worse

You should be grateful

Just you wait, this is nothing

It's about to get so much worse

You aren't a military spouse until
[insert something ridiculous]

I wish I had your life

Just suck it up

living

Sometimes,
all you can do
when you sit in the unknown
is take another breath.

And that is enough.

It means you are living

Military life has pushed me to grow
in ways
I didn't know I could
and in ways
I never wanted.

But also, in ways
I really need

Listen.

When we speak with others,
we first listen
so that we know how
to better take care of them
and how
to better love them.

Listening
is how we connect
and feel closer to others.

So why,
when we
feel within ourselves,
don't we listen?

Each time that I dare to look down
this mountain that I'm scaling,
I smile and see how far I've come,
and know that I'm not failing.

But when I look back up the cliff
the mountain's changed and grown.
How will I ever get anywhere
if my path is always unknown?

45

Of all the acronyms
and strange turns of phrase,
normal
is not a word
in the military's vocabulary

The one
consistent aspect
of military life is
inconsistency

47

Service
cannot exist
without
sacrifice

When you first hear them say
"hey, I just got my orders,
we'll be leaving in May
and we'll have to cross borders"
allow yourself space
to grieve and to mourn.
Please grant yourself grace;
recognize what you've borne.

They're why you remain;
your reason for dealing.

So first comes the pain,
but then comes the healing

Moving isn't just relocating.

It's finding new doctors,
it's learning new roads,
it's making new friends,
it's remembering zip codes.

You fix or toss items
that were ruined on the way,
and say goodbye to friends
who begged you to stay.

It's starting over fresh
and it's longing for "home".
It's finding new adventures
wherever you're forced to roam.

So moving is not just relocating,
it changes who you are.
And you learn that it's about who you're with,
and not the "where you are"

50

Why is it
that I must
experience
to truly,
deeply,
fully
understand?

It is both a blessing
and a curse

Our experiences are shared
in name alone.

You are not me
and I am not
you

Comparing my life
to the woman next door
has only hurt me
and nothing more.

If I only knew
the real trials she faces,
I'd realize that I
never want to switch places.

So I put on my blinders
and focus on me.
What I have is enough.
This is what I choose to see

What do we gain when we suffer?

Often, I have battled with this question. Here's
what I know:

When we suffer,
we gain experience,
we gain knowledge,
and we gain empathy for others
who have suffered
as we have.

But we never could
offer that understanding
if our own suffering
wasn't first received

I often think back
to that five-minute friend
whom I met long ago
and might not see again.

She showed up in my life
when I least expected
I was lonely and hurting
and feeling rejected.

I poured out my heart
to this stranger I met
and somehow felt safe
as my tissues got wet.

She sat and she listened
and had no obligation
to tend to my needs
in this one-sided conversation.

And yet there she was
without judgment or spite.
We soon parted as friends
that may never reunite.

I hope one day I'll be

someone's five-minute friend,
and give them that space
to break and to mend

When I'm told that
joy
cannot exist without
sorrow
I think I finally understand

Along with
the seam-bursting
bubble-popping
explosive
joy

I must have
the light-sucking
core-piercing
violent
sorrow

Resilience.

What a paradoxical word.

While we use it
to flaunt strength,
it also inherently contains
painful circumstances.

In order to be resilient,
you first must be
stretched and
tested and
bent

There are times when I love
what this lifestyle has given me.

I'm immensely grateful for the
blessings I've seen.

And then there are times when
I count down the
days
weeks
years
until their commitment
to the military
is up

My eyes found you
in a sea of uniforms
and now
I can finally
breathe

After so many nights of
sleeping alone,
I sometimes reach out
just to touch you
so I know
you're here

After so many days
of missing them,
they finally come home
and it's not what you'd expect.

Instead of their piece
perfectly fitting back in
to your family puzzle,
the empty space
where they used to be
has slightly
morphed.

You try shoving it
back into it's place,
but your family puzzle
isn't the only thing
that's changed.

Their piece
changed too

There are some moments
as we try to reunite
where living was easier
when I was alone at night

For my friendships that stretch over oceans
or through miles and miles of land,
I miss you and wish you were here with me,
and I hope that you can understand -

Some days I long for my family,
and some days I hate the unknown.
Some days I feel like I'm drowning,
but some days I thrive on my own.

Some days I wish you could just stop by
so we don't have to talk on the phone.
But I've also learned that I have the strength
to do it on my own

No one on this earth
can truly understand
what I've been through.

Part of that is isolating
but part of it is
empowering.

No one can take away
my knowledge
of what I've experienced
or tell me I'm wrong.

There is strength in being me

Is it strange
that I'm grateful for the hard?

Of course
I laugh
and instantly deny
feeling gratitude
while I'm hurting.

But after escaping
I somehow feel grateful
for the lessons
the experience
the calluses

Am I the only one
constantly in distress
from the frequent life changes
with no time to process?

Is the problem just me
and my impatient heart
that can't find a good rhythm
and doesn't want to restart?

Or could others feel this
and they just don't know how
to put thoughts into words
that they're grieving the now?

Will that peace be attained
and leave me feeling whole
or is change a needed step
to a well-lived soul?

I stop to
process the unknown future
that lies before me.

But the present doesn't
stop
to let me process

I've allowed myself time
to feel the pain.

But it's exhausting
and lonely
and I don't want
to sit with it
anymore.

I'm ready

thriving

73

Military life
has taught me
more about myself
my strengths
my weaknesses
my limits
than I would have learned otherwise

The best part
about military life
is also the worst.

Change.

Facing constant change
is undeniably difficult.

But it also teaches you
to say I love you often,
to cling to the moments you have together,
and to prioritize
what is truly
important

Just like
a happy life
has hard days,
so too
does a thriving life
have surviving days

76

It won't take one day,
but there will come a day
when it doesn't feel
so new anymore

Joy may seem far away
like it can only be reached
once a certain goal or
moment happens.

But I think
joy is always around us.

We may choose to ignore it,
and instead revel in sorrow.

Or it may appear
just barely out of reach;
something we can see
but can't seem to touch.

But it's always there.

Even if we ourselves
have a hard time seeing it

She is
the air encompassing you
yet somehow you forgot
that she existed.

Breathe her in
deeply
fully
and then send her
back into the world

- gratitude

79

Today we tried something new.

It's within these moments
that I'm grateful
for the extra push
to try new things
as we explore
new places

As I pass through
each new adventure,
it's true, I drop
little pieces of my
heart.

I scatter them
as I move through
my journey.

And yet,
I am not
empty.

I am overflowing with
little pieces that
others have dropped.

Like that dinner we were given.

The midnight emergency babysitting.

The text that read "hey I'm just checking up on
you".

The extra sets of hands as we unloaded our moving

truck.

Yes, I have left little pieces of me
behind.

But I am made whole again
by the
pieces of others

I thought I was happy
where I was,
but then I learned
that it's not about the where,
it's about the who

There's a unique
instant
understanding
that comes with
military friendships.

You carry each other.
You rely on each other.
You thrive and grow with each other.
You share frustrations, wins, and losses with each
other.

You become family

Those moments
that I look forward to
for months
never go as planned.

But in that moment,
nothing else matters

It finally hits me,
and happy tears
pour down my cheeks.

It's over.

I get you back now

I'm here lying in bed
with a smile so huge
that my cheeks hurt
and I cannot contain the
joy I feel
as I finally can
hold your hand
again

I know it may not make sense
but I really am
grateful
for this
military lifestyle.

I will always have
a deep sense of
gratitude
for the people who serve
and the families that sacrifice

The frequent moves
come with hardship, yes,
but also come
with a stronger
family unit,
and stronger bonds
with friends
that become family

Broken down boxes,
pictures on the wall,
restocked fridge and pantry,
a local friend to call.

The first time you run the dishwasher,
or sleep in your own bed.
Finding a favorite grocery store,
or organizing your shed.

It's starting to feel like home

It is possible
to mourn what you'll never have,
and yet,
still love what you've been given

She's been through
4 deployments and
4 moves in
4 years.

She can share what she's learned,
but that doesn't make her
better or worse
than you.

Own your story

It is not wrong
to feel sad while they're gone.
You don't have to be strong
as the long days drag on.

It is not wrong
to feel joy while they're gone.
Keep moving along,
love isn't withdrawn.

It is not wrong
to get help when you need it.
I know you're headstrong,
so hold that, then release it.

It is not wrong
to do all of the things.
If you're still feeling strong,
see what else life brings.

It is not wrong
to feel all this together;
to feel boundless emotions.
There is no tether.

93

It is not wrong.
All feelings belong

Instead of chasing
the most digestible version of yourself
for the comfort of others,
choose to exist
exactly as you are

Who would I be
without the hard?

Because I know loneliness,
I can truly know belonging.

Because I know heartache,
I can truly know love.

Because I know isolation,
I can truly know community.

Because I know surviving,
I can truly know thriving

affirmations

I am allowed to feel
however I want
about military life.

I am not alone
on this military journey.

I am loved and supported.

I do not need to have
all the answers.

I am more than
just
a milso.

I choose to have compassion
over comparison.

I have strength in me.

I can choose to have peace as I
sit in the unknown.

about the author

Sarah Curtis is the creator of the popular blog *A Military Wife's Life*, which validates military loved ones through the highs & lows of military life.

She holds many titles such as mother, Air Force wife, small business owner, poet, and artist.

Sarah specializes in modern artwork designed to capture memories and beautify your home.

Connect with Sarah at amilitarywifeslife.com,
on social media @amilitarywifeslife,
or through her Spouse-ly and Etsy shops.